Traverse Theatre Company

While You Lie

By Sam Holcroft

Cast

Helen	Pauline Knowles
Ana	Claire Lams
Chris	Steven McNicoll
Edward	Andrew Scott-Ramsay
Ike	Leo Wringer

Director	Zinnie Harris
Designer	Alex Lowde
Lighting Designer	Lizzie Powell
Sound Designer	John Harris

Company Stage Manager	Gemma Smith
Deputy Stage Manager	Dan Dixon
Assistant Stage Manager	Naomi Stalker

First performed at the Traverse Theatre
Friday 30 July 2010

A Traverse Theatre Commission

THE TRAVERSE

Artistic Director: Dominic Hill

The Traverse has an unrivalled reputation for producing contemporary theatre of the highest quality, invention and energy, and for its dedication to new writing.
(Scotland on Sunday)

The Traverse is Scotland's New-Writing Theatre. From its conception in 1963, it has embraced a spirit of innovation and risk-taking that launched the careers of many of Scotland's best-known writers including John Byrne, David Greig, David Harrower and Liz Lochhead. It is unique in Scotland in that it fulfils the crucial role of providing the infrastructure, professional support and expertise to ensure the development of a dynamic theatre culture for Scotland. It commissions and develops new plays or adaptations from contemporary playwrights, producing, on average, six Traverse Theatre Company productions or co-productions per year. It also presents a large number of productions from visiting companies from across the UK. These include new plays, adaptations, dance, physical theatre, puppetry and contemporary music.

The Traverse is a pivotal venue in Edinburgh and this is particularly the case during the Edinburgh Festival – positioned as it is between the Edinburgh Festival Fringe and the Edinburgh International Festival. The Traverse programme overall won twenty-two awards in 2009. It is also the home of the Manipulate Visual Theatre Festival, the Bank of Scotland Imaginate Festival and the Traverse's own autumn Festival.

A Rolls-Royce machine for promoting new Scottish drama across Europe and beyond. (The Scotsman)

The Traverse's work with young people is of major importance and takes the form of encouraging playwriting through its flagship education project, Class Act, as well as the Young Writers' Group. Class Act is now in its twentieth year and gives school pupils the opportunity to develop their plays with professional playwrights and work with directors and actors to see the finished pieces performed on stage at the Traverse. The hugely successful Young Writers' Group is open to new writers aged 18–25. A new project, Scribble, offers an after-school playwriting and theatre-skills workshop for 14–17 year olds. Both programmes are led by professional playwrights.

Traverse Theatre, Scotland's New Writing Theatre
10 Cambridge Street, Edinburgh EH1 2ED

CHARITY NO. SC002368

COMPANY BIOGRAPHIES

John Harris (Sound Designer)

John's work for the Traverse: *Any Given Day, The Dark Things, The Nest, Knives in Hens, Anna Weiss, Family, Perfect Days, Greta, Sharp Shorts, Kill The Old Torture The Young, The Last Witch* (co-produced with Edinburgh International Festival); *Lucky Box, The Garden* (co-produced with Òran Mór). Other theatre work includes: *Monaciello* (Tron Theatre/Naples International Theatre Festival); *Nobody Will Ever Forgive Us, Nasty Brutish and Short, The Dogstone, Julie, Mary Queen of Scots Got Her Head Chopped Off, Gobbo* (National Theatre of Scotland); *Mother Courage, Jack and the Beanstalk* (Dundee Rep); *Jerusalem* (West Yorkshire Playhouse); *Midwinter, Solstice* (Royal Shakespeare Company). Opera includes *Death of a Scientist* (Scottish Opera 5:15 series); *Sleep Sleep/What is She?/The Sermon* (Tapestry Opera Theatre). Film and television work includes: *The Fingertrap* (Bafta Scotland Emerging Talent Award 2009); *Saltmark* (Blindside); *The Emperor, The Green Man of Knowledge* (Red Kite). John was for several years assistant organist at St Giles' Cathedral, Edinburgh, and took his Masters degree in composition at the RSAMD in Glasgow.

Zinnie Harris (Director)

Zinnie Harris is a playwright and theatre director. Her plays for the Traverse include: *Fall* and *The Garden* (co-produced with Òran Mór). Work for other companies includes: *Julie* (National Theatre of Scotland); *Midwinter, Solstice* (Royal Shakespeare Company); *Nightingale, Chase* (Royal Court); *Further than the Furthest Thing* (Royal National Theatre/Tron Theatre/Tricycle Theatre); *By Many Wounds* (Hampstead Theatre); *The Panel* as part of the 'Women, Power and Politics' season (Tricycle Theatre); and a new version of *A Doll's House* (Donmar Warehouse). She has won numerous playwriting awards including the Peggy Ramsay Award, the John Whiting Award, Scotsman Fringe First Awards and an Arts Foundation Fellowship. TV work includes: *Born with Two Mothers, Richard is my Boyfriend* (Channel 4) and episodes for *Spooks* (BBC 1). Directing work includes: *Julie* (National Theatre of Scotland); *Midwinter, Solstice* (Royal Shakespeare Company); *Gilt* (7:84); *Dealer's Choice* (Tron Theatre); *Master of the House* (BBC Radio Four); *Cracked*. Zinnie was Writer in Residence at the Royal Shakespeare Company from 2000–2001, and is currently an Associate Artist at the Traverse Theatre.

Sam Holcroft (Writer)

Sam's work for the Traverse: *Cockroach* (co-produced with National Theatre of Scotland, nominated for Best New Play by the Critics' Awards for Theatre in Scotland 2008, shortlisted for the John Whiting Award,

2009) and *London Street Sauna*. Work for other companies includes: *Pink* as part of the 'Women, Power and Politics' season (Tricycle Theatre); *Vanya*, her radical adaptation of *Uncle Vanya* (Gate Theatre); *Ned and Sharon* (HighTide Festival, 2007); *Vogue* (Royal Court). From 2003–05 she was a member of the Traverse Theatre's Young Writers' Group. She received the Tom Erhardt Award for up-and-coming writers in 2009, and was the Pearson Writer in Residence at the Traverse Theatre, 2009–10. Sam is currently under commission to the Traverse Theatre, Clean Break and Paines Plough.

Pauline Knowles (*Helen*)

Pauline's work for the Traverse: *Gorgeous Avatar, Heritage, The Trestle at Pope Lick Creek, Solemn Mass for a Full Moon in Summer, Knives in Hens, The Speculator*. Other theatre work includes: *Bear on a Chain, Tir na Nog* (Òran Mór); *Cinderella, Othello, Yellow Moon, Wizard of Oz, Don Juan, Liar* (Citizens Theatre); *Man of La Mancha* (Royal Lyceum Theatre, Edinburgh); *Tutti Frutti* (National Theatre of Scotland); *Vassa* (Almeida); *Shining Souls* (Old Vic); *Macbeth, Medea* (Theatre Babel); *Martha* (Catherine Wheels); *A Scots Quair* (T.A.G.). Television work includes: *Garrow's Law, Personal Affairs, Man Hunters* (BBC); *Taggart* (ITV).

Claire Lams (*Ana*)

Theatre work includes: *Educating Rita* (Watermill Theatre); *Absent Friends* (Watford Palace Theatre); *The Miracle, DNA, Baby Girl* (National Theatre); *Faustus* (Headlong Theatre Company); *Fabulation* (Tricycle Theatre); *Presence* (Plymouth Theatre Royal); *Harvest* (Royal Court); *Chimps* (Liverpool Everyman); *Citizenship* (National Theatre Studio); *Fields of Gold, Soap* (Stephen Joseph Theatre); *Coming Around Again, Huddersfield* (West Yorkshire Playhouse); *The Happiest Days of Your Life* (Manchester Royal Exchange Theatre); *The Dice House* (Birmingham Stage Company); *Romeo and Juliet* (Shakespeare in the Park). Film work includes: *Pumpkin Head IV* (Clubdeal PH Film Company); *Southwalk the Movie* (T-Max Media); *Danielle, Sputnik* (London Film School). Television work includes: *The Bill* (Thames Television); *Doctors, Holby City, Silent Witness, EastEnders* (BBC); *The Brief* (Granada).

Alex Lowde (Designer)

Alex studied Drama at Hull University before completing the Motley Theatre Design Course. Design work for theatre includes: *The Elephant Man* (Best Design, Critics' Award for Theatre in Scotland, 2010), *Beauty and the Beast* (Best Design, Critics' Award for Theatre in Scotland, 2009), *A Doll's House, Sleeping Beauty, Equus, Beauty and the Beast* (Dundee Rep); *The Marriage of Figaro* (Sadlers Wells/Ascoli Piceno); *Paradise Moscow* (Royal Academy of Music); *Triptych* (Cambridge University);

Angelic to *Alnwick* and costume design for *Romeo and Juliet* (Newcastle Playhouse). Alex has also worked with Paines Plough and Finborough Theatre. Opera work includes: *The Lion's Face, The Nose* (The Opera Group and ROH2); *The Adventures of Mr Broucek* (Opera North and Scottish Opera co-production); *The Gentle Giant* (Royal Opera House Education); *Candide* (Buxton Festival); *The Threepenny Opera* (Richmond Theatre). Film work includes: *Beyond the Rave* (Hammer Horror/Puregrass films). In 2007 Alex was selected as part of the UK team exhibiting at the Prague Quadrennial with his designs for *Tobias and the Angel*, which opened the newly rebuilt Young Vic.

Steven McNicoll (*Chris*)

Steven is an actor and playwright. Work for the Traverse: *Gordon Brown: A Life in Theatre, Empty Jesters* (Herald Angel Award, 1998) and *Grace in America*. Other theatre work includes: *Trumpets and Raspberries, Vanity Fair, The Merchant of Venice, Tartuffe, Laurel and Hardy, Look Back in Anger* (Nominated for TMA Best Supporting Actor), *The Taming of the Shrew, The Playboy of the Western World, Beauty and the Beast, The Comedy of Errors, Glengarry Glen Ross* (Royal Lyceum Theatre, Edinburgh); *The Mystery of Irma Vep* (Royal Lyceum Theatre, Edinburgh/Perth Theatre); *The Corstorphine Road Nativity* (Festival Theatre, Edinburgh); *Of Mice and Men, Humble Boy* (Perth Rep); *Cinderella, Sleeping Beauty, Aladdin* (King's Theatre, Glasgow); *Dead Funny* (Borderline Theatre); *The Government Inspector, The Steamie* (Pitlochry Festival Theatre, winner of the Leon Sinden Award, 2003); *The Hypochondriac, Le Bourgeois Gentilhomme* (Dundee Rep); *It Had to Be You, The Last of the Lairds, Carlucco, The Queen of Hearts* (Fifth Estate/Hampstead Theatre); *Shanghaied* (Nippy Sweeties); *Aladdin* (Brunton); *Waiting for Godot* (3 Phase). Film and television work includes: *Empty, Legit, Velvet Soup, Rab C Nesbitt, Brotherly Love, Athletico Partick* (BBC); *The Return of Peg Leg Pete, Cry for Bobo* (Forged Films); *Soldier's Leap, Mr Morris, The Life of Jolly* (BBC); *The Ring of Truth* (Channel 4). Radio includes: *Fags, Mags and Bags, The Voyage of the Demeter, From Abstraction, McLeavy, The Passion of Plum Duff, The Lady and the Law, The Franchise Affair* (BBC Radio 4); *Parade's End* (BBC Radio 3); five series of *Velvet Cabaret*. Steven has also co-written plays with Mark McDonnell. Their plays include *There are Such Things* (Winner of the Hamilton Deane Award, 2001) and an adaptation of *The Mouse That Roared* (BBC Radio 4). Steven's first solo play *The House* will premiere at Òran Mór in November 2010.

Lizzie Powell (Lighting Designer)

Lizzie trained at LAMDA. Her lighting work for the Traverse includes: *Any Given Day, The Dark Things,* The Debuts season, *Rupture* (co-produced with National Theatre of Scotland). Other theatre work includes: *Huxley's*

Lab (Grid Iron); *Treasure Island* (Wee Stories); *Transform Glasgow, Transform Orkney, Mary Queen of Scots Got Her Head Chopped Off, Our Teacher's a Troll, Rupture, Venus as a Boy, The Recovery Position* (National Theatre of Scotland); *First You're Born* (Plutôt la Vie); *Pobby and Dingan, The Book of Beasts* (Catherine Wheels); *Under Milk Wood* (Theatre Royal, Northampton); *The Death of Harry, Making History* (Ouroborous Productions, Dublin); *The Wasp Factory* (Cumbernauld Theatre); *The Wall* (Borderline Theatre); *Second City Trilogy* (Cork Opera House); *Smallone, Romeo and Juliet, This Ebony Bird, Tricky* (Blood In The Alley Productions); *Drenched* (Boiler House Productions); *The Night Shift* (Fuel Productions). Lizzie was assistant to the Lighting Designer on *Billy Elliot* at the Victoria Palace Theatre, London.

Andrew Scott-Ramsay (*Edward*)

Andrew trained at the RSAMD in Glasgow. His theatre work includes: *Othello, Cinderella, Yellow Moon* (Citizens Theatre); *Six Characters in Search of an Author* (National Theatre of Scotland); *Carthage Must be Destroyed* (Theatre Royal, Bath). Film and television work includes: *Book of Blood, Merry Christmas, Doctors*.

Leo Wringer (*Ike*)

Leo went to the Guildhall School of Music and Drama where he was awarded the Shakespeare Prize. Theatre work includes: *King Lear, Romeo and Juliet, The Comedy of Errors* (Royal Shakespeare Company); *Julius Caesar* (Barbican); *Medea* (Abbey Theatre, Dublin); *Julius Caesar, The Taming of the Shrew, Othello, Titus Andronicus* (Shakespeare at the Tobacco Factory, Bristol); *Sanctuary* (Royal National Theatre); *Two Horsemen* (Bush Theatre, Time Out Award); *Divine Right* (Birmingham Repertory Theatre); *Search and Destroy* (Royal Court). Film and television work includes: *Silent Witness, Judge John Deed, The Bill, Rough Crossings, Canterbury Tales, Casualty, Rebus, The Kitchen Toto*.

SPONSORSHIP AND DEVELOPMENT

We would like to thank the following
corporate sponsors for their recent support

New Arts Sponsorship Grants
Supported by the Scottish Government
In conjunction with

A&B
Arts & Business Scotland

HIGHLAND SINGLE MALT
SCOTCH WHISKY

LUMISON

Heineken

SCO++ +CO

habitat

pinnacle
communications

To find out how you can benefit from being a Traverse Corporate Sponsor, please
contact Fiona Sturgeon Shea,
Head of Communications, on 0131 228 3223 or
fiona.sturgeonshea@traverse.co.uk

The Traverse Theatre's work
would not be possible without the support of

Scottish
Arts Council

BRITISH
COUNCIL

·EDINBVRGH·
THE CITY OF EDINBURGH COUNCIL

For their generous support, the Traverse thanks our Devotees
Joan Aitken, Stewart Binnie, Katie Bradford, Fiona Bradley,
Adrienne Sinclair Chalmers, Lawrence Clark, Adam Fowler, Joscelyn Fox,
Caroline Gardner, John Knight OBE, Iain Millar, Gillian Moulton, Helen Pitkethly,
Michael Ridings, Bridget Stevens

Emerging Playwright on Attachment post supported by Playwrights' Studio, Scotland
as a Partnership Project

Pearson Playwright supported by **Pearson**

For their continued generous support of Traverse productions, the Traverse thanks:
Habitat, Camerabase, Paterson SA Hairdressing, Stems Florist

For their help on *While You Lie* the company would like to thank:
passITon – giving donated computers to people with disabilities,
Lesley Wilson, Mark & Fran Shaw, Matt Padden, Paulina Nowak,
Euro Business Solutions www.eurobs.co.uk, Paul Claydon (NTS),
Oxfam Books, Stockbridge

TRAVERSE THEATRE - THE COMPANY

WHILE YOU LIE

Sam Holcroft

Characters

ANA, *female, twenties*
EDWARD, *male, twenties*
CHRIS, *male, forties*
HELEN, *female, forties*
IKE, *male, any age*

Note on costume

At no point should any actor appear naked. Where it is indicated that a character undresses, it must either be out of sight of the audience, or they must wear a vest or petticoat underneath their clothes.

Note on accent

Not being a native English speaker, Ana works hard to perfect her accent, often repeating words.

Special thanks to Zinnie Harris, Dominic Hill, Katherine Mendelsohn and all at the Traverse Theatre, Mel Kenyon, Tom Erhardt and Rachel Taylor.

This text went to press before the end of rehearsals and so may differ slightly from the play as performed.

Scene One

ANA's bedroom.

The room is very small and inexpensively decorated.

ANA and EDWARD are dressing to go out for the evening.

ANA wears a red dress. EDWARD changes out of a pink shirt into an evening shirt.

EDWARD. Ana.

ANA. Just a second.

EDWARD. Ana.

> *She looks in the mirror; she smoothes her stomach in her red dress.*

> Ana?

ANA. I'm just going to try the black.

EDWARD. This is fine.

ANA. '*Fine*'?

EDWARD. It's gorgeous. Wear this.

ANA. I'm just going to try the black again.

> *ANA steps out of the red dress and climbs into the black. She wears a full-length petticoat underneath. EDWARD, now dressed, checks his watch.*

EDWARD. Ana?

ANA. Hang on.

EDWARD. We're late, Ana.

ANA. Can you not hang on for a minute?

EDWARD. Forty minutes, Ana, *forty* minutes.

ANA. One more minute won't matter.

EDWARD sighs. ANA looks at herself in the mirror in the black dress.

EDWARD. Okay?

ANA. I look fat.

EDWARD. Ana.

ANA. I look fat in this.

EDWARD. Ana, please.

ANA. Do I look like I've put on weight? Edward?

EDWARD. No.

Beat.

ANA. I need to try the red again.

ANA holds up the red.

I don't look *fat* in the red.

EDWARD approaches her.

EDWARD. You look like you, in red, in black, in nothing... and always beautiful.

Beat.

ANA. Okay. I'm sorry. Why don't you get me some earrings and I'll just be. One. In the...

She points to a jewellery box.

... In there. Yes.

EDWARD opens the jewellery box and fishes around inside.

ANA climbs back into the red dress.

EDWARD. What am I looking for?

ANA. Just find me a pair of earrings that will go with my dress.

EDWARD. Which dress?

ANA. Just any old pair.

> EDWARD *passes her a pair of earrings.*

No. They're not right. Give me another.

> EDWARD *passes her one earring.*

And the other one. Find the other one.

> EDWARD *struggles with a clump of tangled jewellery.*

EDWARD. Why don't you keep them together?

ANA. These are perfect. I need the other one.

EDWARD. It's not here.

ANA. It must be there.

EDWARD. What about these?

> EDWARD *offers her yet another pair of earrings.*

ANA. No.

EDWARD. Why not?

ANA. They look cheap.

EDWARD. They look the same so put them in your ears.

ANA. No. I don't want to look cheap in front of your friends.

> *Beat.*

You go ahead. I'll get the bus.

EDWARD. You can't.

ANA. I'll meet you there.

EDWARD. You can't get the bus in a dress.

> ANA *starts to undo her dress.*

Ana!

ANA. *I can't decide.*

EDWARD. *Why can't you decide?* Red dress. Black dress. I've seen you in both, I've seen you out of both; you only have two dresses.

Beat.

I didn't mean it like that.

ANA. I'm sorry that I can't decide which one of my *only two* dresses makes me look less *fat*.

EDWARD. You know I didn't mean it that way.

ANA. I'm sorry that I can't afford to buy more dresses to look expensive like your friends.

EDWARD. My friends don't care about that.

ANA. They look at me like I'm secretary.

EDWARD. You are a secretary.

ANA *stalks back to the mirror, still in the red dress.*

Ana...?

ANA. If I wear the black I look fat; but the red is too short it shows my legs.

EDWARD. Then show your legs.

ANA. I don't want them to see my legs.

EDWARD. Then stay as you are.

ANA *looks at herself again in the mirror.*

Can we go now?

ANA *puts on her shoes.*

Are you ready?

EDWARD *picks up his wallet and keys.*

Let's go.

ANA *stares at her reflection.*

Ana?

ANA *takes a face-wipe and begins to wipe the make-up off her face.*

What are you...? Ana, no, don't do that.

ANA *smears her make-up with the wipe.*

Don't do this again, Ana, please.

EDWARD *approaches her in urgency.*

You have to get up this close.

He kneels and peers at her thighs.

ANA. Edward, don't.

EDWARD. This close before you can see any veins, I promise.

ANA *covers her thighs, embarrassed.*

ANA. But *you* see them.

EDWARD. How many times can I tell you *I* don't care, okay? I'm not even looking at them, I'm looking at your beautiful hips, and tits and your bum, your flesh, not the skin on your thighs; I'm looking at the bits I can hold on to. Okay, okay?

ANA. Are you saying I'm fat?

EDWARD. What?

ANA. You hold on to my fat?

EDWARD. Everybody has *some* fat, Ana.

ANA. I look fat in this dress, finally you tell me.

ANA *turns away from him. Exasperated,* EDWARD *pockets his wallet and keys.*

Edward?

EDWARD *turns towards the door.*

Where are you going?

EDWARD *opens the door.*

You're going to leave me?

EDWARD. What do you want me to do! If you think you're fat, you probably are, don't ask me; you ask me for a lie.

Beat.

ANA. What? What did you say?

EDWARD. Can we not do this now? Can we just go to the party?

ANA. No, we can't just go to the

EDWARD. I don't want to have this conversation now.

ANA. When do you want to have this conversation, Edward? When would be good time for you to tell me that you think reassuring me is same as lying to me?

EDWARD. Isn't it?

ANA. No!

EDWARD *turns toward the door.* ANA *follows him.*

How long have you been 'reassuring' me for then, huh? All our relationship? Why then? Why didn't you just

EDWARD. The alternative is not worth the hassle; I give the cookie to the dog.

ANA *slaps him hard.* EDWARD *puts his hand to his stinging cheek.*

I long to be honest with you but you're so sensitive that I have to watch everything I say.

ANA. You should have just been

EDWARD. Everything, Ana. And when we fuck I'm thinking too much and I can't.

ANA. You want to fuck someone else? That what you saying?

EDWARD. Ana!

ANA. You want to go fuck someone else? Just be honest with me. Tell me the truth.

EDWARD. The truth?

ANA. Yes, the truth. You coward!

EDWARD. Fine, it's not your varicose veins that make you unattractive, it's your constant begging for reassurance that makes me want to fuck other people.

ANA. Get out. Get out of my apartment!

EDWARD *leaves*.

ANA *stands in shock. After a moment she picks up his pink shirt and holds it to her face.*

Scene Two

CHRIS*'s office.*

The room is large and expensively decorated.

CHRIS *is on the phone at his desk.*

CHRIS. Yes, we did receive your package, yes...

CHRIS *searches on his desk for the brochure.*

... But I haven't had a chance to go through it in any great detail, so now is not perhaps the time to discuss it...

ANA *enters with a tray of coffee. She wears* EDWARD*'s pink shirt from the previous scene. She brings the tray of coffee to* CHRIS*'s desk and sets it down.*

Yes, it does sound a competitive rate, but as I said...

ANA *pours milk into his coffee and places it before him. He smiles to her in thanks.*

... As I said, I haven't had a chance to look in any great detail... Yes, that's right...

CHRIS *rips open a sugar sachet and empties it into his coffee. He discards the packet; it misses the bin. ANA moves to the side of his desk and picks up the packet, putting it in the bin.*

CHRIS *looks at her as she bends over.*

I mean, absolutely. You've hit the nail on the head right there.

ANA *straightens up and moves away.* CHRIS *clicks his fingers at her, motioning towards his jacket hanging on the door. He points to the jacket pocket and beckons to himself.*

So why don't you leave it with me and we can pick up at a later date once I've had a chance to review… the figures, yes… Sure. Yup.

ANA *takes his wallet out of his jacket pocket and brings it to him.*

No, great, great. I'll have my secretary call you and fix a time.

CHRIS *smiles at ANA and gestures his frustration.* ANA *smiles in sympathy.*

Yup. No, we have your card.

CHRIS *finds the business card in his wallet.*

That's all fine. Okay now, sure, great talking to you. Bye now.

CHRIS *hangs up; sighs.* ANA *smiles.* CHRIS *notices a small box on the tray of coffee.*

You got it. This it?

ANA *nods and smiles.*

Great, thank you. What did you go for?

ANA. Perfume.

CHRIS. Great, great choice.

He opens the box and lifts out a small bottle of perfume. He reads the label around the neck.

'Perfection'.

ANA. It's new.

CHRIS. Here, let me smell.

He beckons for her wrist.

Do you mind?

ANA. No. Of course.

She offers him her wrist. He sprays it. He smells her wrist; lingers a second too long.

CHRIS. Perfect. Thank you.

ANA. I was hoping if I could talk to you about my pay review.

CHRIS. Yes, I'm sorry, we will. I know it's been…

CHRIS *finds a receipt in his wallet.*

ANA. Yes.

CHRIS *offers the receipt to* ANA.

CHRIS. And we will, I promise, but just this moment could you run out and pick up my shirts, please?

ANA *takes the receipt.*

ANA. Yes, of course. But can we also talk about my review?

CHRIS. Yes, we will, but I need you to get my shirts before my three o'clock.

CHRIS *checks his watch.*

And can you get me some salmon sashimi? I have to eat before this meeting.

ANA. No problem, but if we have a time in the calendar then

CHRIS. Don't you want to write it down? Shall we write it down?

CHRIS *writes on a sticky note.*

I want a salmon sashimi with miso soup and a side of salad. But I don't want it from the stand outside the restaurant. You have to go into the restaurant and ask at the front desk – otherwise it's not fresh. So go into the restaurant to the front desk, not from outside, and ask it to be wrapped as a take-away. Okay?

ANA *takes the sticky note from* CHRIS.

ANA. Sure, okay. I just. I was hoping if we could

CHRIS. I was hoping *that...*

ANA. I'm sorry?

CHRIS. I was hoping *that* we could, not if. And we will, Ana. We will set a time. But you know how things are, don't you?

ANA. Yes, but

CHRIS. Exactly, so let's just be realistic, okay? It's about understanding the current situation, isn't it? It's about understanding how it affects us all, right down the line, all the way down to the bottom, okay? And we all have to make sacrifices. But, but there are things I've been meaning to talk to you about: responsibilities, extra responsibilities.

ANA. Yes?

CHRIS. Yes, each department needs a qualified first-aider.

ANA. A first-aider?

CHRIS. You go on a first-aid course. You learn to

ANA. I know what a first-aid course is.

CHRIS. Yes, and I could nominate you for this department. Would you like that?

ANA. I would like to talk about my review.

CHRIS. And I have told you that we will.

He passes her the business card.

Now, please call this man and have him come in but give him no more than fifteen, twenty max. You never can tell if they're legitimate over the phone.

ANA *puts the business card in the breast pocket of the pink shirt.*

ANA. Sure, it is hard to know if they are genuine.

CHRIS. I'm sorry, what? You have to speak clearly.

ANA. I said don't you just long for honesty, you patronising cunt.

Beat.

CHRIS. Ana...?

ANA. The thing is, Chris, you've overrun my review by three weeks already and I'm really needing promotion.

CHRIS. Ana, you don't speak to me like

ANA *holds up her hand to silence him.*

ANA. Just give me a minute, and you have a minute, I run your diary very careful, so I know. And before I run out and pick up your shirts and your salmon sashimi – from the inside – I just need just one minute, okay, one minute to explain. You see, one day, when I am old and have children and the walls of my vagina are weak and can no longer support a penis, and my breasts are lying flat on my chest, okay, I am going to need financial assets to keep me attractive. So, you can see, economically I must progress. Now two things, yes, stand in my way: first, obvious, I just call you a cunt; second, also obvious, you are a cunt and will not offer to me because I am woman.

ANA *draws her chair closer.*

I am a woman. And you, you are a man. There must be some way for us to cooperate. Surely man and woman have been here long enough to find some way of working together that… profit them both? I am hoping *that* we can come to some kind of agreement, don't you? Let's be honest about what we want. I am pretty certain that there is a way to… forget this thing that I just say.

Scene Three

CHRIS *and* HELEN*'s bedroom.*

The room is spacious, homely and expensively decorated.

HELEN *is heavily pregnant; she brushes her teeth.*

CHRIS *stands in the doorway.*

CHRIS. Sorry, Helen. I was held up.

HELEN. It doesn't matter.

CHRIS. You cooked dinner, and I missed it.

HELEN. Doesn't matter, Chris.

CHRIS. And Amy…?

HELEN. Is asleep.

CHRIS. I should check on her.

HELEN. No, you'll wake her – she was exhausted; you'll see her tomorrow.

CHRIS. I'm sorry. You ate without me.

HELEN. It doesn't matter. Thank you for calling.

CHRIS. I didn't want you to worry.

HELEN. It's never the same as having you here but I always appreciate the sentiment, thank you.

CHRIS *sits. Slowly he takes off his shoes and socks.* HELEN *steps out of her housedress; underneath she is wearing large, shape-defining underwear and pregnancy tights. As she undresses,* HELEN *takes both of their clothes and puts them in the laundry basket.*

Amy had her class trip.

CHRIS. Of course, Amy had her class trip. How could I forget? How was her trip? How... Where... was her trip?

HELEN. They took her class to the dog shelter.

CHRIS. That's right, the dog shelter. I remember you telling me that.

HELEN. They watched the dogs be fed and cleaned, they visited the vet centre.

CHRIS. Oh right. Great. And why, why did they visit the dog shelter?

HELEN. The school is keen to support the local charities.

CHRIS. Oh right. So we paid?

HELEN. Yes.

CHRIS. We paid for our daughter to visit the dog shelter?

HELEN. Yes.

CHRIS. Great. Great.

HELEN *pulls all her hair into a tight-fitting shower cap. She stands in her tights.*

HELEN. She wants to go again.

CHRIS. Again?

HELEN. Yes, she wanted to know more about them, actually, the dogs.

CHRIS. Oh yeah?

HELEN. Yes, she said. She said the funniest thing. You'll love this: she said, 'Mummy, why was one dog carrying another dog like a piggyback?'

CHRIS. Like a piggyback?

HELEN. She asked why one dog was climbing on the back of another dog.

They both laugh. HELEN *takes a tub of eczema cream and smears it around her nose, between her breasts.*

I know, can you believe it! She actually said that and she's only five.

HELEN *exits to the bathroom.*

CHRIS. Well, what did you say?

HELEN (*calling from off*). Well. I mean. What could I say?

HELEN *returns from the bathroom with a length of dental floss. She flosses her teeth.*

You know. She's five. I said. I said. You know, I said it was one dog asserting itself over another.

CHRIS. 'Asserting itself'?

HELEN. Yes, asserting itself.

CHRIS. You said it was asserting itself?

HELEN. Yes.

CHRIS. Why would you say that?

HELEN. What do you mean, '*Why would I say that?*'

CHRIS. Well, why didn't you say it was… playing?

HELEN. Because it wasn't playing, Chris.

CHRIS. No, but it wasn't exactly

HELEN. You weren't here, Chris.

CHRIS. No, but

HELEN. You weren't here.

CHRIS. No, of course. You're right, I'm sorry. You said the right thing.

HELEN. Don't tell me I didn't say the right thing.

CHRIS. Of course you said the right thing. I'm sorry I wasn't here.

HELEN. It doesn't matter. I told you it doesn't matter.

CHRIS pulls back the covers as if to get into bed.

Have you been drinking?

CHRIS. What?

HELEN holds a pillow out to him.

HELEN. You'll snore. I've set you up in the spare room. You don't mind, do you?

He looks at her: her hair in a shower cap, cream on her face, and tights up to her waist.

CHRIS. I bought you a present.

HELEN. What?

CHRIS. For your birthday. Do you want it?

HELEN. It's not my birthday for two weeks.

CHRIS. Do you want it now?

HELEN. Why, is it going to go off?

CHRIS. No.

HELEN. Then why would I want it now?

CHRIS. No, okay.

Beat.

HELEN. Chris…?

CHRIS. I want you to know that you're perfect.

Beat.

HELEN. Thank… Thank you.

CHRIS *nods and smiles.*

He takes the pillow and leaves the room.

HELEN *watches him go, perplexed.*

Scene Four

ANA*'s bedroom.*

ANA *is throwing* EDWARD*'s possessions at him across the room. She is still wearing* EDWARD*'s pink shirt.* EDWARD *stands holding a box for his possessions; he watches her, forlorn.*

ANA. I'm sick of your shit being in my house. Your shit is everywhere. You practically move in. You don't even ask me. And now everywhere I go there's your shit. You have… shat in every corner of my home. Everywhere I look I am reminded just how much you… invade my life.

ANA *throws some clothes.*

Your clothes are on my floor.

ANA *throws some magazines.*

Your car magazines are on my table.

ANA *picks up a mug.*

Your dishes are in my kitchen.

ANA *reads the inscription on the mug.*

'Why does a woman wear white on her wedding day?

So she can match the kitchen appliances.'

This is seriously excellent joke.

It surprise me that this man is only make cups for a living.

She throws the cup. EDWARD *races to catch it.*

EDWARD. Ana?

She opens a plastic bag on the table and furiously pulls out a can.

ANA. Is this your deodorant?

EDWARD. Ana, please look at me.

ANA. This is not my deodorant. This is for problem perspiration. *I* do not have a problem with my perspiration.

EDWARD. Ana, come on, please.

She throws the can on the ground in front of him and picks up something else.

ANA. What is this? Is this yours?

EDWARD. I don't...

ANA. I expect it's yours because it looks *rubbish.*

She throws it at him.

I was late. Aren't you going to ask me why I was late?

EDWARD *doesn't respond.*

I'm not going to apologise. I was late because I was at the doctor. I was having a smear test; I was making sure you didn't give me a virus. You don't have any symptoms, do you?

EDWARD. No.

ANA. Good. Then we should be clear; my boss doesn't want his wife to catch anything. Is this your apricot facial scrub?

ANA *holds it up for him to see.*

EDWARD. What did you say?

ANA. Well, it's not mine.

EDWARD. Are you having sex with your boss?

ANA. Yes. Do you want your toiletries or shall I just throw them out?

EDWARD *throws the box on the ground.* ANA *stops. She turns to him.*

Don't smash my apartment.

EDWARD *glares at her.*

EDWARD. Since when?

ANA. I don't have to tell you.

EDWARD. Since when!

EDWARD *moves towards her, urgently.*

ANA. After we finish.

EDWARD *stops.*

EDWARD. After we finished?

ANA. Yes.

EDWARD. You won't have sex with me for two months but you'll fuck him the week that we finish!

ANA *doesn't respond.*

If it wasn't over before, it certainly is now. Good for you that you got over us so quickly.

EDWARD *aggressively throws his possessions into the box.*

ANA. I had my heart set on you.

EDWARD. And your eyes firmly on the prize.

EDWARD *busies himself filling the box;* ANA *follows him.*

ANA. I had made plans for us! Before you even ask, before you knew, I have plans for us to marry and make children with grandparents who speak different language and eat different food.

EDWARD *turns on her.*

EDWARD. How could you... with him? *Him!* How often did you complain about him?

ANA. I don't have to explain to you

EDWARD. No, fine. Fine. You can explain to him. You can explain to him why you'll only fuck in the dark. Or do you let him look at you? Do you let him get a good look at you? You make him feel welcome, do you? You make him feel wanted.

They look at one another. ANA *doesn't respond.*

Give me back the dress.

ANA. What?

EDWARD. I want everything that's mine.

ANA. You gave it to me.

EDWARD. I want everything I paid for. Give me back everything that I paid for.

ANA *fetches the red dress off the rail. She passes it to him; he takes it. They look at one another.*

You're wearing my shirt.

ANA *looks down at herself. She takes off the pink shirt and passes it to him.*

She stands in her vest.

ANA. It smells of me.

EDWARD. It's still mine.

ANA. Promise to wash it.

EDWARD. I will not.

They stare at one another.

ANA. I will let you know the results of my sexual health screen.

You can let yourself out.

ANA *exits the room.*

EDWARD *stands with the box.*

After a moment, he lifts the pink shirt out of the box. He smells it, buries his face in it. He stops, rummages in the shirt pocket and withdraws the business card placed there in the previous scene. He turns it over in his hands.

Scene Five

CHRIS *and* HELEN*'s kitchen.*

HELEN *sorts the dirty laundry from the washing basket into colour-coordinated piles for the wash.*

The doorbell rings. HELEN *opens the door.*

EDWARD *stands on the other side.*

EDWARD *is wearing the pink shirt returned to him by* ANA *in the previous scene.*

EDWARD. Hi.

HELEN. Hello.

EDWARD. We've met.

HELEN. We have?

EDWARD. Yes, we have.

HELEN. We have, yes, I recognise you.

EDWARD. I came to your summer barbecue.

HELEN. Yes, I remember.

EDWARD. I came with

HELEN. You came with Ana, that's right. Edward, isn't it? You'll come again? It's by open invitation.

Short pause.

Won't you... come in?

EDWARD. Thanks.

EDWARD follows HELEN in and looks around.

HELEN. How is Ana? She's a great girl, isn't she? Chris just couldn't do without her.

EDWARD. We broke up.

HELEN. Oh.

Beat.

I'm sorry.

Short pause.

EDWARD. You have a lovely home.

HELEN. Thank you, that's kind of you.

EDWARD moves into the space. HELEN watches him cautiously.

But really this kitchen is so dated.

EDWARD. It's got great proportions.

HELEN. Hasn't it? That's why I love it. Though it does make us responsible for the community social calendar – we are the only ones with a dining space this large. I have so many plans for it. But what with the current climate –

EDWARD. Yes.

HELEN. – it may have to date some more.

Short pause.

Would you like some home-made lemonade?

EDWARD. You make lemonade in your home?

HELEN. Yes.

EDWARD. Wow. I didn't think they made women like you any
more.

HELEN *turns to fetch the lemonade.*

But actually I really can't stand the stuff. Sorry.

HELEN *stops, affronted.* EDWARD *picks up a photograph.*

Is this your daughter?

HELEN. Yes.

EDWARD. How old is she?

HELEN. Five. Five years old.

EDWARD. Difficult age?

HELEN. No, no. She's… well, you know. Just put her in front
of the TV!

HELEN *laughs overenthusiastically.* EDWARD *smiles.*
HELEN *trails off…*

I'm sorry you broke up with your girlfriend.

EDWARD. Yeah, me too. Because I love her.

HELEN. Oh good, I mean

EDWARD. And she asks me to explain why?

HELEN. Yes, why?

EDWARD. Because.

HELEN. What is it –

EDWARD. I just.

HELEN. – about her –

EDWARD. I simply can't.

HELEN. – that you love?

EDWARD. I simply can't explain it. And I don't understand. I
genuinely don't understand.

Why I have to.

Beat.

You see, she needs constant, constant reassurance. She doesn't see what you or I see –

HELEN. No, okay.

EDWARD. – when we look at her.

HELEN. Right.

EDWARD. And she doesn't have her mother here, or many friends. I, I am the only one she talks to and so I'm the only one limiting the damage she's doing in her head and I'm exhausted.

HELEN. Sure, right.

EDWARD *laughs*.

EDWARD. Completely shattered, you know.

HELEN. Uh-huh.

EDWARD. Like I'm walking a knife-edge and I think, I don't know, I'm pretty sure she just pushed me over the edge.

Beat.

You haven't yet asked me why I'm here.

HELEN. Are you hungry, can I get you something to eat?

EDWARD. I'm making you uncomfortable, I'm sorry. It's hot, isn't it?

HELEN. No...

EDWARD *unbuttons his pink shirt*.

I mean, yes, it is hot.

EDWARD *takes off his shirt, he wears a vest underneath*.

EDWARD. I make you uncomfortable.

HELEN. No, I mean, that's fine; you can...

EDWARD. It makes you uncomfortable that I am so honest
with you.

HELEN. No, that, no, of course not. Don't be silly, it's not as
though we are

EDWARD. Strangers.

HELEN. No. I admire… I admire a man who can be…

HELEN *looks at him, his bare arms.*

… honest in this way.

EDWARD. You do?

HELEN. Yes, of course.

EDWARD. I saw you looking at me at your summer barbecue. I
saw you looking at my arms, my hairlessness. I saw you
looking at me like I was your son grown up, but a son you
could fuck.

Beat.

HELEN. Excuse me?

EDWARD. You said you admired honesty. I was looking at you
too.

HELEN *backs away from him.*

HELEN. I think you should leave.

EDWARD. I think there's something I should tell you.

HELEN. Please leave now.

EDWARD. Don't you want to know why I came?

HELEN. I used to have sex with twenty-five-year-olds when I
was twenty-five.

EDWARD. No, that's not why.

HELEN. And now I no longer need to have sex –

EDWARD. Helen.

HELEN. – with *boys*.

EDWARD. No, Helen

HELEN. Just go, Edward, please, you're scaring me!

EDWARD *turns and walks out, leaving his shirt behind.*

HELEN *picks up the shirt. She is about to add it to the laundry when she stops; she lifts the shirt to her face and smells it.*

Scene Six

CHRIS*'s office.*

IKE *sits across from* CHRIS.

IKE. The escalating situation has obviously led to this unprecedented rise in demand. Currently there are few viable options and that's where we come in, we can offer the most sophisticated technologies. We provide the most skilled professionals. So you see, with our annual corporate sponsorship package you can align your company with the most advanced in the field of cosmetology. We are the future of plastics.

IKE *takes out several photographs and rises out of his chair to pass them across to* CHRIS.

Here you will see.

IKE *points at the photograph.*

Before.

CHRIS. Oh...

CHRIS *grimaces in disgust.* IKE *swaps the photograph.*

IKE. And here as well.

CHRIS *winces and turns his head.*

CHRIS. Right, thank you, that's fine. Thanks.

IKE *swaps the photograph again.*

IKE. And after. See? You see the difference?

CHRIS. Yes... great.

ANA *enters with a tray of coffee.*

IKE. We have performed seven thousand charitable reconstruction surgeries in that country alone. I will show you.

IKE *points at yet another photograph.*

CHRIS. Really, that's not necessary.

CHRIS *tries to avoid the photograph.*

IKE. In this particular instance, insurgents blew up a nursery school. Here you can see that the tissue is irreparably damaged.

CHRIS *grimaces again.*

Don't worry, this little girl is in no great pain: the burns are deep into the nerve endings. Our surgeons will apply skin grafts harvested from the lower back and buttocks.

IKE *shows him another photograph.*

Like so, you see?

CHRIS *turns away in discomfort.*

CHRIS. Yes, sure, sure.

IKE. This allows for faces disfigured by burns, wounds, amputations, etcetera, to be really quite satisfactorily restored. And our aftercare programme involves regular medical assessment as poor healing may require a second surgery.

IKE *searches for another photograph.*

An example of poor healing...

CHRIS. Please, really, thank you, but I

IKE. Grafted skin can often shrink over time and create a very unnatural look.

IKE finds the photo and presses it on CHRIS.

CHRIS. Yes, yes, thank you.

CHRIS pushes the photograph away.

IKE. Many of these girls are left unable to eat or speak properly. Often they are not allowed to work or go to school.

ANA pours IKE a coffee.

Thanks. Thank you.

ANA smiles politely. She pours CHRIS a coffee.

Your corporate sponsorship would benefit the world's most unfortunate. We currently offer charitable surgeries in six of the world's war-torn countries.

ANA turns to leave, CHRIS motions for her to stay.

CHRIS concentrates on emptying three sugars into his coffee.

The financials.

CHRIS looks up.

CHRIS. Yes, the financials.

IKE. We run our charity as a not-for-profit division of our corporation. Your annual sponsorship would contribute direct to surgeries with only a small run-off corridor for overheads and administration

CHRIS holds up his hand for IKE to stop.

CHRIS. Sorry to stop you – this all sounds great. A great thing you're doing with your practice.

IKE. Thank you.

CHRIS. But look, Mr...

IKE. Please call me Ike.

CHRIS. Sure, Ike. I would like to look at the figures in my own time. So why don't you just leave. This with my secretary. And she'll...

IKE *stands and holds out his brochure.*

Yes, just, just give it all to her...

IKE. Sure, okay.

CHRIS. Great.

IKE *hands the documents to* ANA *and offers a business card to* CHRIS.

IKE. This is my number if you want to be in touch.

CHRIS *takes the card and puts it in his jacket pocket.*

CHRIS. Sure, she'll be in touch. One way or another.

IKE *looks to* ANA*; she smiles apologetically.*

IKE (*to* CHRIS). Thank you so much for your time.

CHRIS. Sure, no problem. Bye now.

IKE *exits the room.* CHRIS *looks at* ANA. *There is a short pause.*

ANA. Shall I...?

ANA *collects up the photographs on his desk.*

It sounds good... his proposal. It sounds a good thing for the children. I think he seems to be... legitimate, don't you?

ANA *stares at the photographs.*

Oh...

She touches her hand to her lips. CHRIS *walks round the desk and stands behind her. He presses his body into hers.* ANA *looks through the photographs.*

Look at these poor girls...

CHRIS *buries his head in her neck.* ANA *concentrates on the photographs.*

CHRIS. Oh, I've missed your smell. I've been craving to touch you all day.

CHRIS *pulls her shirt down over one shoulder, kisses her neck.* ANA *turns and pushes him back.*

ANA. Wait.

CHRIS. What?

ANA *looks at* CHRIS, *uncertain.*

What's wrong? Don't you want to? I think about you all the time. I don't know what you've done to me. I've never fucked a foreigner before. This feels so… exotic.

He returns to her; he gropes her. ANA *steps back.*

ANA. It's the middle of the day.

CHRIS. I'll lock the door.

CHRIS *hurries to lock the door.*

ANA. There are people outside. Don't you care that there are people outside?

CHRIS *stops.*

CHRIS. Look. Today I was in my car and a woman stopped by my window on her bicycle. She was powerfully muscular, okay? And as the lights changed she powered down on the pedals, the muscles went tight beneath the skin and she took off. And it was…

He tries to find words for the sexuality of it.

It was…

ANA. Why are you telling me this?

CHRIS. It is about weighing up the risk. Even the women I do not fuck are an assessment of risk.

ANA. I am worth the risk?

CHRIS. Yes.

ANA *smiles a small smile.* CHRIS *resumes kissing her neck.*

ANA. I saw this dating programme last night; did you see it?

CHRIS. What?

CHRIS *puts his hands on her.*

ANA. These girls, beautiful girls

CHRIS. Beautiful girls?

ANA. Competing to date a rock star, a big rock star.

CHRIS *slides his hands around her to reach her buttocks.*

CHRIS. Yeah, a big rock star.

ANA. And he was down to the last two.

CHRIS *moves his hands smoothly towards her breasts.*

CHRIS. Two beautiful girls.

ANA. Yes, and their last task was to fuck him.

CHRIS. They fucked him?

ANA. Behind the closed door.

CHRIS *undoes his fly.*

CHRIS. Turn around.

ANA. What?

CHRIS. Put your hands on the desk.

ANA *turns around.*

Put your hands on the desk.

ANA *puts the photograph on the desk and puts her hands either side of it. She looks at it.*

Tell me more about those girls.

ANA. As if a dog bit into her face.

CHRIS. What? Not *those* girls.

> *He shoves the photographs aside.*

> The girls on the television.

ANA. They had to fuck him and then he got to decide.

> CHRIS *hitches up her skirt.*

CHRIS. Lucky guy.

> CHRIS *pushes her into the desk.*

Scene Seven

A park bench.

ANA *waits uncomfortably.* EDWARD *approaches. They greet each other without warmth.*

EDWARD. Hi.

ANA. Hi.

> EDWARD *sits. He fishes in his pocket for a wallet of photographs.*

EDWARD. Here.

> *He hands her the wallet; she takes it.*

ANA. This is all of them?

> EDWARD *nods.*

> What about on your computer?

EDWARD. I deleted them.

ANA. How do I know you deleted them?

EDWARD. Because you asked me to be honest with you, so I am.

They look at one another.

I have to get back to work.

ANA. Hang on.

ANA *takes a seat on the bench. She opens the wallet and lifts out the photographs.*

EDWARD. You don't have to look at them, they're all there.

ANA. I want to look at them.

ANA *gasps and presses the photos to her chest. She looks at* EDWARD *in surprise.*

When was this?

EDWARD. Ages ago.

ANA. I don't remember this exact

EDWARD. Those were the days when you let us do it with the lights on.

ANA *stares at the picture.*

When I could actually see the girl I was having sex with. Do you understand how sad it was for me when you made us do it in the dark? I would have gone down there with a torch between my teeth. When you looked like you did in that picture, with your legs wide open, showing me who you are, I loved you for it.

ANA *looks up at him, embarrassed, alarmed.*

(*Pointing at her.*) But then you started looking at me like that. Just like that, there! Like sex was some kind of ordeal I put you through, telling me it takes too long, telling me to stop looking at you. Do you know how unsexy that is?

Beat.

ANA. I regret sending you that weblink.

EDWARD. What? What weblink?

ANA. When I first meet you. The one on the women health website where you click to see what happen to a woman's breasts when she run without a bra. Or jog or trampoline. I was trying to make you laugh.

EDWARD. What's that got to do with anything?

ANA. I wanted you to laugh at these women. I disgust myself.

EDWARD. That's what you regret? It's not a big deal, Ana.

ANA. Yes, it is.

EDWARD. No, it isn't. The fact that we could never have sex properly, that's a big deal. That's something to regret.

ANA looks at him.

You think the wrong things matter.

ANA. No.

EDWARD. If you are not looking in a mirror, you are covering the mirror with towels and crying about what you saw when you last looked in a mirror. Something is wrong, Ana. You need to get help.

ANA looks away. She looks at the photographs. EDWARD *puts his hands up in surrender.*

I have to go.

ANA. I remember this. You don't have to give back this. I only wanted the ones where I was...

She offers him the photo. EDWARD *doesn't take it.*

You don't even want the ones of Christmas?

EDWARD *doesn't respond.*

Well, I'll leave it here. And maybe somebody will find it and smile because we look so happy.

ANA puts the photograph on the bench beside her. They look at one another. They share a moment of tenderness.

EDWARD. Just stop. Stop having sex with him.

Beat.

Please.

ANA. Thirty hours on a coach I come here.

EDWARD. Ana.

ANA. Four years university and I couldn't get a job where I come from.

EDWARD. I know, but that's no reason to

ANA. I thought I could really be something, you know, really be somebody.

EDWARD. Yes, but that's no

ANA. Thirty hours on a coach I come here. But still I cannot use my education.

EDWARD. Ana, that's no excuse, if you were willing to fuck for a job you should have just stayed at home.

EDWARD *stalks away, leaving* ANA *alone*.

Scene Eight

A really cheap hotel room.

ANA *looks around the room with a growing sense of unease.*

CHRIS *takes off his watch.*

CHRIS. Take your clothes off, Ana. We don't have time to fuck about. I have to be home in two hours.

ANA. Then we should do it with our clothes on.

CHRIS. What is the point of doing it with our clothes on, for me? I might as well put my dick in my fist with you standing by. Take your clothes off; I need to be home on time.

ANA *looks around the room.*

Ana. Hurry up; I'm late.

Beat.

Ana?

ANA. I don't want to take my clothes off –

CHRIS. Why?

ANA. – in here. Could we not have gone to a decent hotel? Is this all I'm worth?

CHRIS. I am not exactly flush with cash, Ana. You may have your promotion, but I haven't had mine. I'm just trying to avoid redundancy here. Now I've paid the hour, stop wasting my time.

ANA *looks at the bed.*

ANA. The rate of suicide in my country is higher than here, did you know that?

CHRIS. What?

ANA. There is no money, no jobs, no purpose.

CHRIS. Ana.

ANA. So if we are unhappy here we can console ourselves that we are not as unhappy as we would be there.

CHRIS. So what are you complaining about? If you went home you wouldn't have a job at all.

ANA. No, I couldn't pay my rent.

CHRIS. Exactly.

ANA. I'd be out on the street.

CHRIS. You should consider yourself lucky.

CHRIS *undoes his belt.*

I won't ask you again, Ana.

ANA. I want responsibility.

CHRIS. What?

ANA. I want responsibilities at work. Not just administration, not photocopying, picking up your shirts, I want to really be something.

CHRIS. You can't just go straight from administration to

ANA. Then I want training.

CHRIS. Who will cover administration while you are training?

ANA. I will have to have my own assistant.

CHRIS. No.

ANA. No?

CHRIS. Don't be absurd.

ANA picks up her coat.

Wait, wait, hang on. I can't get you an assistant. I wouldn't be able to find funds for that.

ANA makes to leave.

But I can train you; I can do that.

ANA turns back to him.

You will have to study at weekends.

ANA nods.

And you will need to improve your English.

ANA. I will improve.

CHRIS looks at her.

CHRIS. Then what more do I get?

ANA. More?

CHRIS. Yes, you want more opportunity then… so do I.

ANA *hesitates a moment before offering.*

ANA. This is not your country.

CHRIS. What...?

ANA. This is my country. Where I come from. Where I cannot pay my rent. Where I am on the street.

CHRIS *begins to nod.*

I am on a street in my country and you, you are...

CHRIS. I am in the car. A car.

ANA. Yes.

CHRIS *continues to nod.*

CHRIS. I brought you to this room.

ANA. A room on a street in my country. I don't know anything about you. You don't know anything about me. I don't even have a name. There is no need to tell the truth; we might never see each other again.

CHRIS. Yes, I am nothing but a man with a car. And you, you are...

ANA. I know what I am.

They look at one another. It is decided.

CHRIS. Take your clothes off.

ANA *looks at him, uncertain.*

Now.

CHRIS *takes off his belt.*

ANA. Chris, I...

CHRIS *comes towards her.*

CHRIS. I don't have a name.

CHRIS *approaches and begins to fasten his belt around her neck.*

I don't have a life outside this room. I have nothing to think of. Tonight is not about *my* struggle.

CHRIS *offers her the belt strap*.

Now bite down.

Scene Nine

CHRIS *and* HELEN*'s kitchen*.

HELEN *hangs out the clean damp laundry onto the clothes horse. She wears the pink shirt left to her by* EDWARD *in their previous scene*.

CHRIS *enters. He looks dishevelled, hollow-eyed. He stares at his wife*.

CHRIS. Darling, I'm sorry. I'm so sorry again.

HELEN. I didn't make you any dinner.

CHRIS. You knew I'd be late.

HELEN. No, I just didn't make you any dinner.

Beat.

CHRIS. I've been working very hard to provide food for you to put on the table.

HELEN. You didn't call.

CHRIS. I didn't have time; I was run off my feet.

HELEN. What about your secretary, was she off her feet too?

Beat.

CHRIS. She had to leave; she had a thing with her boyfriend.

HELEN. Her boyfriend?

CHRIS. Yes.

Beat.

HELEN. Your meeting ran over?

CHRIS *nods*.

Go all right, did it?

CHRIS *shakes his head*.

CHRIS. It was very... unusual.

HELEN. Unusual?

CHRIS. Usually I can... I can strike a balance, you know? But this time, this time I think I may have crossed the line.

CHRIS *steadies himself against the wall*.

HELEN. Chris?

CHRIS. We are in a crisis.

HELEN. Yes.

CHRIS. And people are acting out of character.

HELEN. Yes, but

CHRIS. Because we're, we're under a lot of pressure.

CHRIS *lowers himself into a chair. He takes off his jacket and hangs it over the back of the chair.*

I'm so hungry, Helen.

HELEN. Would you like a biscuit?

CHRIS. I'd love some biscuits.

HELEN *reaches into her pocket and retrieves a biscuit. She hands it to him; he looks at her, perplexed.*

Thank... thank you, darling.

HELEN *nods*. CHRIS *eats the biscuit*.

HELEN. I spoke to Jim Robinson about the hog roast for the summer barbecue, he's going to come with three girls like last year, I said we'd pay them on the day.

CHRIS. Look, I've been meaning to say, do you really think it's necessary to have three waitresses for the party?

HELEN. There'll be over a hundred and fifty guests.

CHRIS. Yes, about that, do we really want to invite that many this year? I think we need to cut costs, don't you?

HELEN. It's for my birthday, Chris.

CHRIS. I know, and I want to celebrate your birthday, but what about a more intimate affair, a supper party, or, or

HELEN. We do it every year, everybody expects it. Besides, don't they say you have to spend your way out of depression?

CHRIS. Yes, but that doesn't apply to a household budget, Helen.

HELEN. Amy's teacher called; I had to pick her up.

CHRIS. Why, was she sick?

HELEN. They said she was 'assaulting' her classmates.

CHRIS. What?

HELEN. Yes. They very firmly said, 'She cannot go around *assaulting* her classmates like that'.

CHRIS. Like what?

HELEN. Climbing on their backs.

CHRIS. Oh, Helen.

HELEN. It's all right, I sorted it out.

CHRIS. You told her the truth?

HELEN. I told her that what she saw was a boy dog asserting itself over a girl dog. I explained that it's only the boys that do the asserting, not the girls.

HELEN *continues to focus on the washing*.

CHRIS. You said what?

HELEN. And so then she asks why, and, and I said because they are animals. And animals don't have equality between the sexes.

CHRIS. Helen

HELEN. Don't worry, I explained it to her in terms she could understand: we are not dogs. We *used* to live like dogs, we *used* to walk on our hands and eat raw meat and carry our children in our mouths. And men used to climb on the backs of women because there was no shelter, no running water, no heat, and they had to keep order to survive. But gradually, as time went by, we began to walk upright, and eat with our hands and we learnt to speak. Now we have supermarkets full of food and central heating and cinemas and men don't need to assert themselves any more because they are civilised.

CHRIS. Helen

HELEN. I said, 'Why don't you ask your daddy? He'll tell you he has no need to assert himself in this day and age.'

  Beat.

CHRIS. I think we should redo the kitchen.

HELEN. What?

CHRIS. I think we should redecorate.

HELEN. You do?

CHRIS. Sure, why not?

HELEN. But you just said that there are costs we can't afford.

CHRIS. I have set aside some funds for our future. This is an investment in our future.

HELEN. Oh, darling, I have so many ideas.

CHRIS. That's what I'm saying.

HELEN. Really?

CHRIS. That's what I'm saying, Helen.

HELEN claps her hands together.

HELEN. Oh, this is brilliant, you brilliant man!

CHRIS. You perfect woman.

They kiss. HELEN tries to engage him in an embrace, but he gently pushes her off.

HELEN. Chris…?

CHRIS. You know I can't…

HELEN. Please, Chris.

CHRIS. When you…

He points vaguely to her pregnant belly.

HELEN. What?

CHRIS. When you're… I'm tired, Helen. I'm really tired. So, I think I'll just bunk in the spare room. You don't mind, do you? Darling?

HELEN. No, of course not.

CHRIS turns to go upstairs.

When he is gone, HELEN suddenly dives upon his jacket and rifles through the pockets. She fingers through receipts and tissues until she comes across IKE's business card; she casts the jacket aside and turns the card over in her hands.

There is a knock at the door. HELEN looks up in alarm. She approaches the door. She doesn't open it.

Hello, who's there?

EDWARD. Helen, it's Edward.

HELEN. Edward?

EDWARD. Yes, I know it's late, but I just wanted to tell you

HELEN. No, I'm sorry, I'm busy.

EDWARD. Helen?

HELEN. Sorry, so so busy. You'll have to go.

HELEN walks away from the door. EDWARD appears at the kitchen window; he tries to open it.

HELEN. Edward? What are you doing?

EDWARD lifts open the window.

EDWARD. Helen?

HELEN. No, no, don't open the window.

EDWARD. Please, Helen, I have to tell you.

HELEN rushes to the window.

HELEN. Keep your voice down, everyone's asleep.

EDWARD. I've been going round and round in my head, Helen, and I think I have a responsibility to tell you.

HELEN tries to close the window; EDWARD struggles to keep it open.

HELEN. No, I said last time

EDWARD. I'm not here to have sex with you

HELEN. Edward, let go.

EDWARD. I don't need to have sex with you.

HELEN. Keep your voice down!

EDWARD. I need to tell you what I know. Don't you want to hear it?

HELEN. Don't you think I might already know!

EDWARD stops struggling. HELEN closes the window on him. After a moment, he walks away.

HELEN looks down at herself in EDWARD's pink shirt. Suddenly she pulls it off in distress and throws it onto the clothes horse with the rest of the washing.

Scene Ten

IKE*'s office.*

HELEN *sits across from* IKE.

IKE *is showing* HELEN *'before' and 'after' photographs of surgeries.*

HELEN. Oh, well, goodness.

IKE. You see?

HELEN. Yes.

IKE. And here?

> HELEN *grimaces.*

HELEN. Oh gosh, gosh.

IKE. While she no longer has the use of her left eye, ear or three of her fingers, we were able to regenerate the skin, like so...

> IKE *produces an 'after' shot.* HELEN *looks at the photograph.*

So at least she now has some semblance of facial symmetry.

HELEN. Right, yes. There's quite a...

IKE. Difference.

HELEN. Yes.

IKE. So you understand? Your husband's corporate sponsorship could help to change the lives of the most unfortunate children.

HELEN. Oh, I'm not here in regards his company's involvement.

IKE. No?

HELEN. No, I don't work for him. I married him.

IKE. Yes, of course.

HELEN. No, I found your card in his pocket.

IKE. I see.

IKE nods in acknowledgement.

HELEN. My husband is...

IKE nods in understanding.

He is... Our nanny is fat; specifically.

IKE. Yes. Of course.

HELEN. I weigh up the risk of my child being fed on chips and chocolate against the risk of my husband wanting to... the nanny.

She laughs nervously.

And the truth, the honest-to-God truth, is that I'd rather my child be fat than not have a father. So I let her. I let her feed my child chocolate bars.

IKE. Yes.

HELEN. Bars of *chocolate*.

IKE. Yes.

HELEN. Do you see?

IKE. I understand.

HELEN. Do you?

IKE. Yes, sure.

HELEN. Can you help me? Could you help me with this situation?

IKE. I could help you. We could help. Fix you up.

HELEN. Please, yes, anything.

IKE. Well…

HELEN. Yes?

> IKE *considers for a moment.*

IKE. To start… we could cut your child out before it reaches your vagina; so you could keep your vagina for him.

HELEN. Oh…

IKE. And then you would feed your child formula so you could keep your breasts for him.

HELEN. Oh, I see, yes…

IKE. And you would follow the baby-food diet to shed the baby weight when not breastfeeding.

HELEN. Yes, okay.

IKE. And when you go out, to restaurants, with friends, you would take this –

> *He produces a small bowl.*

– and be sure never to eat more in one sitting than could fill this bowl.

HELEN. It's so small…

IKE. And finally we would thick your lips with collagen to give you the perfect 'cupid's bow'.

HELEN. Oh yes.

IKE. So that when you are sixty he would still come home to fuck the vulva on your face.

> Okay?

> HELEN *looks at him with wide eyes.*

> It's just a suggestion.

> IKE *stands and moves to his desk. He takes out his selection of leaflets and brochures.*

The payment plan for such treatment, if you want it, is laid out in our financial brochure.

HELEN. Payment, yes, of course. I have come into some money.

IKE. That's wonderful.

HELEN. My husband has written over some money to me for an investment in our... future.

IKE. That's wonderful.

HELEN. Yes, it is.

IKE. Then you may be interested to know that we also offer individual sponsorship packages? For a reasonable price, our individual package can contribute to up to three surgeries per year.

IKE *offers her the photographs once again.*

HELEN. Oh, really I don't...

IKE. Surely you can see we increase the odds for these women –

HELEN. I can, but

IKE. – of finding security.

HELEN. Yes...

IKE. You understand then.

HELEN. Yes, I do, I really do, but I just don't think I could invest my husband's money into your sponsorship package without his consent. Charity shouldn't be forced upon you, should it? Then it would no longer be charity.

IKE. Of course. May I have the small bowl?

HELEN *looks at the bowl.*

HELEN. But.

IKE. Yes?

HELEN. I am considering…

IKE. Yes?

HELEN. The other…

IKE. Suggestion?

HELEN. Investment opportunity that you described.

IKE. Investment opportunity, yes.

HELEN. And I think that is perhaps more suitable. Because…

HELEN *motions to the photographs.*

… things are different here. Here it's not so much about finding a husband as keeping one; do you understand what I'm saying?

IKE *nods.*

And if things continue as they are, my husband may be looking at a fifty per cent asset loss irrespective of the climate. So I think he will see that an investment in, in me, an investment that would circumvent the halving of his portfolio, as a worthy investment indeed. And I am sure he would agree that I have acted with his best interests at heart.

Scene Eleven

The street outside ANA*'s apartment.*

ANA *hurries towards her front door.*

CHRIS *follows in pursuit.*

CHRIS. I didn't think you would mind. I saw it on TV. A programme about people that do that –

ANA. Stay back.

CHRIS. – and the TV is in your house.

ANA. I'm not letting you in my house.

CHRIS. Oh, come on, Ana, it wasn't that bad. Was it?

    ANA *turns on him.*

ANA. What if somebody did that to your daughter?

CHRIS. What?

ANA. What if somebody did

CHRIS. My daughter is five years old.

ANA. What if somebody did that to your daughter when she
was twenty-five years old?

CHRIS. I… I don't know, if that's what she wanted…

ANA. 'If that's what she wanted'?

    ANA *unwinds her scarf, revealing purple ligature marks on
her neck.*

    You ask her, when she's twenty-five, you ask her if that is
something she could ever want!

    CHRIS *stares at her neck in alarm.*

CHRIS. We… we were just playing.

ANA. I've seen dogs play fairer than that.

ANA turns to put her key in the lock. Finally he concedes.

CHRIS. Okay, all right. All right. I didn't expect to take it that far, okay, I didn't expect to take it as far as that.

Beat.

Honestly, Ana, I'm… I'm not used to having that kind of power. I know I took you by surprise; I surprised myself. But… you didn't protest.

ANA. You gag my mouth.

CHRIS. You didn't thrash your arms or kick your legs; you braced yourself. And I… Ana, I…

ANA. Yes?

CHRIS. I enjoyed your humiliation.

CHRIS breathes deeply; he trembles slightly.

Is that really my true self, tell me it's not? Ana?

ANA doesn't respond.

It can't be, no man, no person can be defined by one night, surely? Ana, help me, please, I want to put this right, I want… I want…

ANA. What? I can't hear you. You have to speak clearly.

CHRIS. I want you to urinate on me.

ANA. What?

CHRIS. I want you to urinate on me.

ANA. I heard you. Have you lost your mind?

CHRIS unbuttons his shirt.

CHRIS. I want it. I need it.

ANA. What are you doing?

CHRIS *pulls the shirt open.*

CHRIS. It will redress the balance, Ana.

ANA. You disgust me.

    CHRIS *kneels in supplication.*

CHRIS. I disgust myself. Humiliate me!

    CHRIS *takes his shirt off completely.*

ANA. What are you doing? You can't undress in the street.

CHRIS. Please, Ana, I must surrender to you.

ANA. No.

CHRIS. You can do what you like to me. You might surprise yourself.

ANA. No, Chris, no!

CHRIS. Please!

ANA. No, I don't care, okay? That what you need to hear? I don't care. I set you up.

CHRIS. What?

ANA. Yeah, sure, I set you up. I fuck you for the money so don't feel guilty for tying me up like a whore. Let's just say out loud, that's what I am. And a whore is nothing, right?

CHRIS. Ana...

ANA. You don't need to apologise to a whore, you just need to pay her on your way out. Don't worry about it. After a while it didn't feel like being fucking, it feel like being stabbed. I wanted to be stabbed, Chris, I want somebody to stab me. Again, I want you to stab me again, Chris.

    CHRIS *begins to back away, looking at her in horror.*

Stab me again, Chris, because I'm nothing!

    CHRIS *backs off and away, leaving his shirt behind.*

Scene Twelve

CHRIS *and* HELEN*'s kitchen.*

Amy can be heard crying upstairs.

HELEN *ignores the crying and sits herself at the dinner table. She ties her hair back. She tucks a napkin into her neckline. She empties a pot of baby food into the small bowl given to her by* IKE. *She eats it with a plastic spoon. It is a struggle. She retches.*

There is a pile of clean laundry with EDWARD*'s pink shirt folded neatly on top.*

The key is heard in the lock; CHRIS *arrives home.*

He is wearing a jacket with no shirt underneath.

CHRIS. Hello, darling. I made it home on time.

> HELEN *doesn't look up from her baby food.*

Did you get the flowers? I wanted to apologise for being so late so often, I want you to know I'm going to try really hard not to be so late so often in future. I hope you liked the flowers, I don't really know about these things, I just asked for ones that...

Amy continues to wail upstairs.

Is that Amy?

> HELEN *continues to resolutely eat her baby food.*

Helen, can't you hear her? She's bawling her eyes out up there.

> CHRIS *makes to go upstairs to Amy.*

HELEN. Leave her. It's for her own good.

CHRIS. Helen, what's going on? What did she do?

> HELEN *continues to shovel baby food into her mouth; she speaks as she eats.*

HELEN. Those bloody dogs.

CHRIS. What now, what has she done now?

HELEN. They won't have her back.

CHRIS. What?

HELEN. They won't have her back at school until she can behave properly. Until she stops…

CHRIS. Stops…?

HELEN. Barking.

CHRIS. Barking?

HELEN. Stop repeating what I'm saying, I'm telling you she has been barking at her male teachers.

CHRIS. What, she actually

> HELEN *waves her spoon at* CHRIS.

HELEN. Yes, she actually has been barking at them.

CHRIS. Not the women?

HELEN. No. I explained again, but she doesn't seem to understand, I think she's worried that they will try and assert themselves. But I told her, again I told her, it was a long time ago that they indulged in that sort of behaviour; they don't need to assert themselves in this day and age.

CHRIS. Helen.

HELEN. 'Why?' she says. I said, 'Because times have changed.'

'Why?' she says again. '*Why? Why? Why? Why?*'

I said, 'Don't question me! If the boys are not behaving like dogs then you don't behave like a dog. You behave like a dog and I will treat you like one. I will beat you and kick you and make you eat off the floor.'

HELEN *takes a mouthful and chokes it back.*

CHRIS. Helen, what are you eating?

HELEN. 'You see if you can be master of all the others if you're picking scraps from under their table.'

HELEN *burps and coughs a bit back up.*

CHRIS. Is that baby food?

HELEN. I told her, 'You go back to school and you be good like the other girls'

CHRIS. Why are you eating baby food? You're pregnant. What are you doing?

HELEN. I told her not to worry about men, they're not bad; they're not bad any more.

CHRIS. Helen!

HELEN *looks at* CHRIS.

How did you get from dogs mating to men being bad?

HELEN. I don't know, you tell me.

They meet eyes.

The teacher asked if there was something wrong at home.

She asked if there was something wrong with our marriage.

Beat.

Of course, I told her everything was fine. Everything's fine.

HELEN *resumes eating. She retches and vomits a bit back into the bowl.*

She looks at it.

CHRIS. Helen…

HELEN. You're not wearing a shirt.

CHRIS. No...

> HELEN *passes him* EDWARD*'s pink shirt from the top of the pile of laundry. He takes it.*

HELEN. The chairs have arrived for the summer barbecue.

> HELEN *gives the bowl a stir and continues eating.*

Scene Thirteen

IKE*'s office.*

ANA *sits across from* IKE.

IKE. Well, yes, of course, militancy-related injuries are not just facial, are they? Guns and bombs aren't the only explosive devises used as weapons of war – rape is a most effective tool of destroying communities. We can really help to minimise genitourinary trauma. The lingering damage should hopefully only be psychological.

ANA. Psychological?

> IKE *hands* ANA *some more leaflets.*

IKE. Yes, there are many associated psychosocial issues that we also help to address: self-concept.

ANA. Yes, yes, that.

IKE. When the girls are young they will often share the same self-concept as their peers, but as they grow older, being different can become very alienating.

ANA. Yes.

IKE. Leading to feelings of shame, isolation, heartache.

ANA. Yes. Yes. Yes.

IKE. So you understand?

ANA. Yes. How could you not?

   IKE *knocks the table in satisfaction.*

IKE. Precisely, yes, how could you not! Your boss, he agrees with you?

ANA. Oh. I'm sure he does.

IKE. Yes.

ANA. But that's not why I'm here.

IKE. No?

ANA. No, he's very busy at the moment; you know how things are.

IKE. Of course.

ANA. I'm sure when things have settled down…

IKE. Of course. Did you know that we also offer individual sponsorship packages? Your charitable contribution can invest directly into a better future for these women.

   IKE *pulls out some more leaflets.*

ANA. I read your literature.

IKE. On individual sponsorship?

ANA. Yes, all of it. I read that this little girl can put her tongue through the roof of her mouth and into her nose.

IKE. Yes.

ANA. And a thought come into my head that some men may want to put their dick in a mouth like that and up into a nose. You know, for something new. But maybe the ugliness would stop him and she would be spared that… indignity, or maybe, maybe she would want it. And then I have to remind myself that she is only a child with no roof to her mouth. Sorry.

IKE. Not at all. It's clear you understand: for women especially, any injury to the face is disastrous.

ANA. How do you address the, as you say, 'psychosocial issues'?

IKE. There are several avenues we could pursue.

ANA. Yes?

IKE. Behavioural therapy. Medical treatments.

ANA. Yes, do you have something medical? Because, you see, I
    think there is something wrong with my

IKE. Teeth?

ANA. No.

IKE. Your lips –

ANA. No.

IKE. – are very thin.

ANA. No, my brain. I think there is something wrong with my
    brain.

IKE. You do?

ANA. I keep watching these films.

IKE. Films?

ANA. Porn films.

   IKE *nods*.

   These images are in my head now.

IKE. Sure.

ANA. And I have this… dream. This dream again and again.

IKE. Recurring dream.

ANA. I give birth. And in my dream I then try to have sex with
    my baby. I wake up and I cry, hysterical, and, Edward, he
    never understood what was the matter because, of course, it's
    only a dream.

   But these images they are everywhere: in the street, on the
   train, on the television and now they're in my brain. Do you
   see?

IKE. I see.

ANA. And, and I think I may have made a mistake.

> IKE *continues to nod.*

> But if I think for too long I feel sick. And I'm sick so much already that my teeth are turning yellow.

IKE. We can fix that.

ANA. And the only way to stop is to stick tweezers in my thigh. But the scars, they look like veins.

> Every day I count the veins and I find it harder and harder to sleep.

IKE. Yes, I can see.

ANA. There is an arrhythmia in my chest, I'm sure of it.

> IKE *nods in appreciation.*

> I toss and I turn, but feel…

> *She puts* IKE's *hand on her heart.*

> … How irregular.

> IKE *continues to nod in acknowledgement as he moves his hands to lift her breasts and shape them.*

IKE. Sure, okay.

ANA. Do you think it might be broken?

IKE. Sure, sure. I could help fix you up.

ANA. Please. Can you help?

IKE. I could help –

ANA. Please.

IKE. – cut some symmetry here.

ANA. Yes.

IKE. And here.

ANA. Yes.

He pulls the skin of her face taut.

IKE. And smooth away much of the inconsistency you are experiencing.

ANA. It has been so inconsistent.

IKE *spreads her lips with his fingers.*

IKE. I could take you back to before the irregularities began.

ANA. Please. Yes, please.

ANA lies back in the chair as IKE works his way back down her body; he lifts her legs, pulling them apart and reaches up into her groin.

IKE. It would be as though it never happened.

ANA. Yes, please.

IKE. I would cut it out.

ANA. Yes.

IKE. And with the pieces –

ANA. Yes.

IKE inserts his fingers into her vagina.

IKE. – I would sew you a hymen. And restore you.

ANA. Yes.

IKE. And you would heal.

ANA. I would heal.

IKE. You would heal.

ANA. I would heal. Yes.

IKE withdraws his fingers and moves to the desk. He takes out a clipboard and forms.

ANA collects herself in the chair.

IKE. The payment plan for such treatments, if you want them, is laid out in our financial brochure – shall I also include a form for individual sponsorship?

ANA. Well, I'm not sure that...

IKE. You are no longer a secretary, is that right?

ANA. No, I am an Executive Assistant now.

IKE. That's wonderful.

ANA. Thank you. But the extra really doesn't go that far. So, really, I couldn't do both.

IKE. No?

ANA. No, I couldn't. Do both.

IKE. You must choose one or the other.

ANA. Yes.

IKE. People need to be happy. That's why plastic surgery is important; it makes them feel normal.

ANA. Yes, I just want to feel normal.

IKE. Then really it's no choice at all.

ANA. No.

Scene Fourteen

CHRIS*'s office.*

CHRIS *and* EDWARD *face each other across the room.*

CHRIS *wears* EDWARD*'s pink shirt.*

CHRIS. I haven't seen you here in a while.

Beat.

Ana is having her lunch.

EDWARD. Good for her.

CHRIS. Yes, she told me you two were no longer a couple.

EDWARD. She told me you two were fucking.

Beat.

CHRIS *pushes his chair back and stands up.*

CHRIS. All right, Edward, what do you want?

Did you come here to punch me, is that it?

CHRIS *walks out from behind his desk.*

Is that it, Edward, you want to punch me in the face? I could punch you back. I could punch you back in the face; you know that?

Is that what you want, for us to punch each other in the face here in my office?

EDWARD *moves towards him.* CHRIS *steps back in alarm. They almost circle each other.* EDWARD *stops.*

EDWARD. Your shirt?

CHRIS. What?

EDWARD. It's nice.

CHRIS *looks down at the shirt.*

CHRIS. You want it? I don't even know why I'm wearing it. My wife lays it out; I put it on. I don't even like pink. You want it, it's yours.

EDWARD *shakes his head.*

EDWARD. No. You keep it.

CHRIS. Then what? We're both civilised men, are we not? There's a way for us to cooperate. Surely we can come to some kind of agreement that will profit us both?

CHRIS *takes out his chequebook and makes out a cheque for* EDWARD.

You see, though times are tight, I had ring-fenced some money for an investment into my home. But I think that a reallocation of funds will convince you to overcome this thing that you have been told.

CHRIS *offers the cheque to* EDWARD.

You fill in your name.

Scene Fifteen

IKE's *office*.

EDWARD *sits across from* IKE. *He is turning over the business card in his hands.*

EDWARD. I found your card in her pocket and I'm concerned that she might come to you for treatment.

IKE. I can't talk about my other clients.

EDWARD. So she is a client of yours?

IKE. I'm afraid that's confidential.

EDWARD. Sure, okay, but tell me, do you have any checks in place, checks to spot people who are seeking physical change as remedy for a psychological problem?

IKE. We assess all of our clients' needs, of course.

EDWARD. Good, because then you would have seen that nothing about her needs changing, only the way she sees herself.

IKE. Often the most effective remedy is to change what people see, yes.

EDWARD. No.

IKE. I'm afraid I can't discuss another client's case.

Beat.

Is that the only reason you came?

EDWARD *looks at the floor.*

We offer a wide range of services: liposuction, mentoplasty, facial implant?

EDWARD. No... Thank you.

EDWARD *makes to stand*.

IKE. We do a line in non-surgical procedures if you prefer?

EDWARD *stops*.

Hair-loss treatments? Laser hair removal? Botox injection?

EDWARD. No, I...

IKE. Yes?

EDWARD. I have a...

IKE. Yes?

EDWARD. I have a problem with...

IKE. Ejaculation?

EDWARD *recoils in embarrassment, he nods*.

EDWARD. Yes.

IKE. Sure, okay.

EDWARD. I can...

EDWARD *raises his arm to indicate an erection*.

IKE. Have an erection.

EDWARD *nods, acutely embarrassed*.

EDWARD. Yes... yes, I can. I can... go for hours.

IKE. Okay, sure, okay.

EDWARD. It chafes. Us both. I... ache.

IKE *nods in sympathy*.

All the time. I am exhausted. I don't know if, if it's me, or, or if it's her, I don't know if I will always...

EDWARD *breaks off in distress*.

IKE. Sure, it's okay.

IKE *beckons for him to unzip his trousers;* EDWARD *does so.*

EDWARD. I tried to punch a man today. Her boss, I tried to punch him.

IKE. Ana's boss?

EDWARD. Yes, but I couldn't do it. Maybe I am *entirely* impotent.

IKE *reaches into his trousers to examine his penis.*

The thing is I have to... cum. That is the truth. One way or another. It doesn't matter if I'm inside. Or out. I must... cum. *I must cum.* This is the fact: if I couldn't fuck I would blow myself up.

IKE *masturbates* EDWARD. EDWARD *cums very quickly.*

After, IKE *stands and moves to his desk. He cleanses his hands before taking out brochures.*

EDWARD *collects himself and does up his flies.*

How much do I owe for the... consultation?

IKE. There is no charge.

EDWARD. Oh. Thank you. For your time.

IKE *nods and smiles.*

IKE. However, might I bring your attention to the charitable division of our corporation? We offer individual sponsorship packages for our charitable cause. We run a programme to

EDWARD. Sure.

IKE. I'm sorry?

EDWARD. Sure, of course. I have just come in to some money.

IKE. You have?

EDWARD. Yes.

IKE. That's wonderful.

EDWARD. Yes. I suppose it is. You must have it all for your charity.

IKE. All of it?

EDWARD. Yes, you must have it all.

IKE. Well, thank you. Thank you very much. Don't you even want to know of the cause?

EDWARD *offers the cheque given to him by* CHRIS *in the previous scene.*

EDWARD. Does it matter?

IKE *smiles and takes the cheque from* EDWARD.

You fill in your name.

Scene Sixteen

CHRIS*'s office.*

CHRIS *sits at his desk.*

EDWARD*'s pink shirt hangs over the back of his chair, along with another dirty shirt and a tie.*

ANA *enters carrying a takeaway carton of sushi and a pot of miso soup.*

CHRIS. Ana

ANA. Salmon sashimi and a miso soup.

CHRIS. Thank you, Ana, you didn't have to

ANA. Do you have anything for dry-cleaning?

CHRIS. No, I

ANA. What about these?

ANA *swipes the shirts off the back of the chair.*

CHRIS. Ana, really, you don't need to do that. I... I...

> ANA *looks at the pink shirt. She turns it over in her hands.*

I'll get Helen to do it, Ana; you don't have to

ANA. I always do it, Chris, what's changed?

> *Beat.*

Your two o'clock is here.

CHRIS. What? I don't have a two o'clock.

ANA. I put it in your diary, I told you I would.

> ANA *opens the door to the office;* IKE *is standing on the other side. She smiles at him.*

Come in.

CHRIS. Ana...?

> IKE *extends his hand to* CHRIS.

IKE. Ike, remember? I came to see you, do you remember?

> CHRIS *doesn't take his hand.*

CHRIS. Ana, I don't have time for this.

ANA. You do have time, Chris, I made sure of it.

> ANA *turns to* IKE.

Enjoy your meeting.

CHRIS. Ana?

IKE (*to* ANA). I'll see you next week.

ANA. I can't wait for it.

CHRIS. What? Why will you see her next week?

ANA. Goodbye, Chris.

CHRIS. What...?

ANA *exits the room, closing the door behind her.*

(*To* IKE.) I'm sorry...

IKE. Ike.

CHRIS. Ike, sure, could you just give me a moment?

IKE. You don't think it's important that we maximise the time we have together?

CHRIS. Sure, but I

IKE. I wondered if you'd had time to think more about our corporate sponsorship package? We offer competitive rates and it's a very good cause, don't you think?

CHRIS. Look, it's not that I don't think it's a good cause. Because I think it's a good cause.

IKE. You can say it.

CHRIS. I just don't think that

IKE. It's all right, say it.

CHRIS. I. We are in a position to

IKE. Say I am a black man.

CHRIS. What?

IKE. It's all right, you can say it.

CHRIS. What? I'm, sorry? I mean... I didn't notice.

    CHRIS *laughs uncomfortably.*

IKE. It's all right, you can say it.

CHRIS. No, no, no. You. You've got me all wrong. I. I. I... there's no need... I mean. I'm not. Not like that. What?

IKE. Just say it, Chris. They're just words.

    CHRIS *laughs again.*

CHRIS. What? No, no. I don't. I don't need to say anything. I'm fine with

IKE. Say I'm a black man, Chris.

CHRIS. F... Fine. I mean, fine. I didn't realise. You... Of course. Whatever you want. If you want. You're a black man.

IKE. No, no. Say '*I* am a black man'.

CHRIS. What, me? No. no. I'm not. A black man.

IKE. Just say it, Chris. It's just an exercise that we do. Part of the individual sponsorship package. You need to just say it, Chris; just relax, say it, and see how it feels. Come on now. It's only words. Say 'I am a black man'.

CHRIS. No.

IKE. Come on.

CHRIS. No.

IKE. Come on.

CHRIS. No. This is. This is. I am a black man.

CHRIS *laughs nervously.*

IKE. There you go. See, it was easy. Now say 'I am a black woman'.

CHRIS. What? What, this is silly. This is really silly.

IKE. Sure. It's hard. I know. Some people can't do that.

CHRIS. It's not that I can't.

IKE. No.

CHRIS. It's just that I

IKE. Won't. Sure. That's okay. We'll leave it there.

IKE *stands and closes his folder.*

CHRIS. No, I mean...

CHRIS *laughs again; he holds up his hands in surrender.*
I'm a black woman.

IKE. 'I'm a black woman with facial injuries.'

Beat.

'I am a black woman. With facial injuries.'

Beat.

Say it.

Beat.

The sooner you say it, the sooner this is all over and done. Say it.

CHRIS. I am a black woman with facial injuries.

Beat.

IKE *smacks his palm with his fist.*

IKE. There you go! Chris, there you go.

See? Now you know!

CHRIS *lowers himself into his chair.*

Now you know how it feels. To say that.

IKE *pats him on the back.*

How do you feel? Come on. Tell me how you feel.

CHRIS. I feel.

IKE. Yeah?

CHRIS. I feel a bit light-headed.

IKE. Yeah? That's okay. That's normal. Put your head down. That's it. Bend your head.

CHRIS *bends his head between his knees.*

IKE *produces a document.*

Sign here. Yes, yes. Just. That's it. Just here. Bend your head.

CHRIS *signs without looking.*

We made progress today. Well done. Big progress.

IKE *gathers the signed documents and backs out of the room.*

We'll be in touch with your payment plan. Okay? We'll be in touch.

CHRIS *nods without lifting his head.*

You're the man, Chris. Aren't you?

CHRIS *lifts his hand in acknowledgement without looking up.*

You're the man.

IKE *goes.*

Scene Seventeen

CHRIS *and* HELEN*'s kitchen.*

HELEN *plates up for the summer barbecue. Guests can be heard outside in the garden.*

She sharpens a large carving knife.

CHRIS *enters.*

CHRIS. Helen, where's Amy? I want to run the egg-and-spoon. Helen?

HELEN. She's not coming.

CHRIS. What?

HELEN. She's not running the egg-and-spoon.

CHRIS. Why, what's wrong with her?

HELEN. '*Wrong with her*'?

HELEN *laughs a little hysterically.*

CHRIS. Helen?

HELEN. Do you have any idea what the other mothers are saying about her, about our daughter? It's bad enough that we had to cut back on waitresses; do you realise the effect that has had on the atmosphere? They were looking to us for assurance, they were looking to us to show them that things don't have to change.

HELEN *pulls a chicken thigh off with her hands and slaps it down on the platter.*

CHRIS. Helen, please.

HELEN. They have been so looking forward to this, a day off from having to worry about the future, and what do they get instead? They have to offer to help handing around the canapés. They just want some normality.

HELEN *sweeps her hair out of her eyes, smearing chicken juices on her face.*

And if that wasn't bad enough, now my daughter is barking at their husbands.

CHRIS. Helen.

HELEN. They're saying I have raised my child to run wild.

CHRIS. Darling.

HELEN. They are saying I have given her no civility.

CHRIS. They're not saying that.

HELEN. They're thinking that we are not civilised people any more.

CHRIS. Helen, come on

HELEN. Are we not civilised people, Chris? Are we not?

HELEN *sniffs the chicken thigh in her hand. She is about to bite into it, but instead tries to stuff it into the small bowl from the previous scene.*

CHRIS. Helen…?

HELEN *concentrates on squashing the chicken into the bowl.*

Darling…? I got you a little gift.

HELEN. Huh?

CHRIS. Just a little birthday gift.

HELEN. A present?

CHRIS. Yes.

CHRIS *offers her a wrapped box.*

Happy birthday.

HELEN *takes hold of the box with a free hand. She shakes it.*

Darling, careful.

HELEN. What is it?

HELEN *shakes the box again.*

CHRIS. Helen. Helen, are you drunk?

HELEN *unwraps the box with her free hand.*

CHRIS *tries to take the small bowl.*

Do you want me to

HELEN *holds the bowl and chicken aloft, waves him away.*

HELEN *manages to get the perfume out of the box.*

HELEN. Perfume.

CHRIS. Yes, it

HELEN *sprays the air. She sniffs.*

It reminded me of you. See, see what it's called…

HELEN *reads the label.*

HELEN. Huh.

HELEN *sniffs again. She sniffs the bowl. She tries to squash more chicken into it.*

CHRIS. Helen, darling, the money, the money for the kitchen.

HELEN. The chicken?

CHRIS. No, the kitchen. The money for the *kitchen*.

HELEN. Yes.

CHRIS. I need it back.

HELEN. What?

CHRIS. I've had second thoughts over the value of an investment in the house. And, well… I've… well, I've gone and made an alternative investment.

HELEN. You what?

CHRIS. On our behalf, darling. I have invested elsewhere. Believe me, it is a very good investment. It is protecting our future. Together.

HELEN. You can't.

CHRIS. I have, darling. I had to. I had to make a quick decision, a snap judgment.

HELEN. No, you don't understand.

CHRIS. And I really want you to trust that I made the right decision.

HELEN. No –

CHRIS. For us.

HELEN. – you can't have it back. I spent it already.

CHRIS. What? On what?

Beat.

HELEN. Charity.

CHRIS *balks.*

CHRIS. Charity?

HELEN. Yes, darling.

CHRIS. You… You gave my money to charity?

HELEN. Yes, I gave it all to that man. That man who helps the little children with the disfigured faces.

CHRIS. You… What?

HELEN. The man who helps the children, darling.

CHRIS. The man who came to my office?

HELEN. Yes.

CHRIS. You gave… You gave *him* my money?

HELEN. Yes, him, I gave it all to him.

CHRIS. Helen… that was. My money.

HELEN. You can't be angry with me, it's for charity.

CHRIS. Yes, but charity shouldn't be forced upon you.

HELEN. No, but don't you agree that a willing contribution is really no charity at all? Because you will always be rewarded by your own sense of selflessness.

Having crammed the bowl, HELEN *begins to eat the contents.*

To be truly generous, one must suffer the loss, as you are now, and the knowledge that your loss will greatly benefit others will give you comfort, and you will make your peace with it, and in that end, darling, you will know true, true charity. Don't you agree?

ANA has appeared in the doorway.

ANA. Hi.

CHRIS swings round to face her. ANA is once again wearing the pink shirt she took from CHRIS in their previous scene.

CHRIS. Ana!

ANA. Hello.

CHRIS. What are you doing here?

> HELEN *aggressively eats the chicken.*

HELEN. Don't be rude, Chris. The summer barbecue was by open invitation.

CHRIS. Yes, but I didn't know you were coming. I'm so glad you're here.

HELEN. I'm so glad too, I've never been so glad.

ANA. I won't stay long; I just came to tell you that I am leaving. The company. I quit.

HELEN. You're leaving?

CHRIS. What?

ANA. I have already handed my notice in to HR.

HELEN. What a shame!

CHRIS. You can't

ANA. Yes, I can, and I have.

CHRIS. No, I need you

> HELEN *aggressively eats the chicken.*

ANA. Chris

CHRIS. I need you to work for me.

ANA. No.

CHRIS. I can't work without you.

ANA. You can. And you will.

> I have to go.

HELEN. Bye-bye now!

> HELEN *tears at a chicken thigh with her teeth.* EDWARD
> *appears.*

CHRIS. Please, Ana, just hang on a second

HELEN. Edward

ANA. Yes, he

HELEN. Is here. Why are you here, Edward?

  ANA *turns to* EDWARD.

ANA. Edward...?

EDWARD. I heard the summer barbecue was by open invitation.

HELEN. No. I changed my mind.

EDWARD (*to* ANA). You won't answer my calls. You won't answer the door.

CHRIS (*to* EDWARD). She doesn't want to speak to you.

EDWARD. I didn't know where else to find you.

CHRIS. We had an agreement, Edward.

ANA. What agreement?

EDWARD (*to* CHRIS). I am confused; who did we agree I wouldn't speak to?

ANA (*to* CHRIS). Why are you speaking to my boyfriend?

EDWARD (*to* ANA). I'm your boyfriend?

  ANA *and* EDWARD *look at one another.*

CHRIS. Ana, Ana, don't look at him like that

  HELEN *starts to breathe heavily and erratically.*

  Both men vie for ANA's *attention.*

EDWARD. Ana, I need to talk to you.

CHRIS. Don't look at him like that, Ana.

HELEN. Chris... Chris...?

CHRIS. Ana, seriously, you don't want to be with a guy like him.

EDWARD. Ana?

HELEN. Please, Chris.

CHRIS. Hang on a second, Helen. Ana, seriously, this guy came to my office.

EDWARD. Just come and talk to me, Ana.

CHRIS. I didn't tell you, he came to my office like some crybaby.

HELEN. Chris…

CHRIS. Just a second, Helen.

EDWARD. Come away and talk to me, please.

CHRIS. Ana, don't listen to this guy – this schmuck – is

HELEN. Chris.

EDWARD. Ana?

CHRIS. This *schmuck* is…

HELEN. Telling the truth!

>   HELEN *bellows in pain. She is in labour. They all turn to her in alarm.*

CHRIS. Helen!

HELEN. No, oh no… No… I can't.

CHRIS. What is it, Helen? Is it time?

HELEN. No, it can't. Not yet. I'm not ready.

CHRIS. It's okay, Helen, we've done this before.

HELEN. No, no, I need Ike.

CHRIS. Ike?

ANA. Ike?

HELEN. Somebody get Ike, please, he's in the garden.

EDWARD. Why is Ike in the garden?

HELEN. *The summer barbecue was by open invitation!*

    EDWARD *goes to fetch* IKE.

CHRIS. Why do you need Ike?

HELEN. No, no...

CHRIS. What's the matter, what's wrong?

HELEN. It can't come yet, no, no!

CHRIS. Helen...?

    HELEN *wails in pain.*

    EDWARD *returns followed by* IKE.

    They all avoid meeting his gaze.

HELEN. Ike! Ike, please, help me

    IKE *bends beside* HELEN *and feels under her dress.*

IKE. Easy now.

    I'm here, it's okay.

CHRIS. Hey, what the fuck are you doing?

IKE. I can already feel the head.

HELEN. No.

IKE. We won't make it to the hospital in time.

HELEN. No! What about my investment? I might as well have given it to charity.

CHRIS. Helen...?

HELEN. Tell me there's something you can do.

IKE. There is something.

HELEN. Anything!

CHRIS. What are you talking about, you said you did give the money to charity?

HELEN *turns to* CHRIS, *imploring him.*

HELEN. No, I lied, I lied to you. Only because I didn't know how to explain the truth. I invested in us, in the security of our future together. Tell him, Ike.

IKE *nods.*

IKE. That's right, you mustn't be angry; she has made some very brave plans to invest in the future of your family. We had plans to remove the baby by way of the stomach and thereby safeguard your future as a couple.

CHRIS. What?

IKE. Just listen to me. Listen to me carefully. Spend on your marriage now, save in the long term. Do you understand what I'm saying? If we make a small cut here...

IKE *motions to her belly.*

... it will mean fewer cuts later on, do you understand me?

CHRIS. No, I...

HELEN. Chris, Chris, look at me. You don't have time to think about it, you just have to accept that this is the right thing for us.

CHRIS. I, I don't need you to...

HELEN. Don't you? You don't need it, really?

CHRIS *can't respond.*

If we do this we stand a good chance. You want us to have a future together?

CHRIS. Of course, yes.

HELEN. Then I need you to trust me.

CHRIS. I...

HELEN. Do you trust me?

Slowly CHRIS *nods,* HELEN *turns in earnest to* IKE.

IKE. Everything's going to be all right. Let's get you lying down.

HELEN. Thank you.

IKE *motions to the crockery on the table.*

IKE. Ana, can you clear the table, please. Quickly.

HELEN *lies on the kitchen table.*

There we go.

She cries in pain.

I know. I know.

EDWARD (*to* ANA *in a whisper*). Come on, let's go.

IKE. Edward, I need water and kitchen towel.

EDWARD. What?

IKE. Lots and lots of kitchen towel.

EDWARD. But I…

IKE. No you don't, do you, Edward?

IKE *fixes* EDWARD *a look.* EDWARD *concedes and goes to the side to collect the kitchen towel.*

ANA. Edward?

IKE. Ana, will you hold her?

ANA. What? No, I…

IKE. Don't shy away, now, Ana, you will need to be brave for your turn. Come and hold her, please.

ANA *reluctantly moves towards the table to hold* HELEN *down.*

That's it, like that.

CHRIS. Is this… Ike, is this safe?

IKE. The world over, women have been operated on without anaesthetic.

CHRIS. But here, here we always use anaesthetic.

IKE. It's nothing new. Now, we need something for her to bite down on. I don't want her chewing her tongue.

HELEN. Your belt, Chris, give me your leather belt.

CHRIS *looks down at his belt in horror.*

IKE. That will do nicely. Chris?

HELEN *nods and smiles at* CHRIS *encouragingly.*

HELEN. What we both want.

HELEN *helps* CHRIS *to undo his belt. She bites down on the leather strap.*

IKE. Nicely done. Now hold her.

They hold her.

Hold her very steady.

All three of them look at IKE. IKE *brandishes the kitchen knife. He looks at the three of them.*

Something wonderful is about to happen. Aren't you all glad you're here?

Using the knife, IKE *cuts into her womb and pulls out her baby. The baby cries its first breath.*

A boy! It's a boy!

CHRIS. A boy. I have a boy!

IKE. You have a boy!

CHRIS *climbs onto the table with* HELEN; *they embrace with elation.*

ANA *and* EDWARD *begin to back away.* IKE *turns to them.*

I'll see you next week, Ana?

ANA *slowly shakes her head.*

Ana?

ANA *and* EDWARD *take hands and together they back out of the room as* CHRIS *climbs atop his wife and penetrates her undamaged cunt.*

Scene Eighteen

ANA*'s bedroom.*

EDWARD *undresses her from the pink, now bloodied, shirt. He is careful and tender. She wears a white vest underneath the shirt. He scrunches the dirtied pink shirt in his hands and discards it on the floor. They are silent.*

He produces a clean white shirt, unfolds it and begins to dress her in it. Again, he is gentle and tender. She allows him to dress her. She sniffs the arm of the shirt, inhales its freshness. She watches him, full of regret.

ANA. We had sex nine times. I want you to know.

EDWARD. Ana.

ANA. I want you to know I didn't like it.

EDWARD. It's all right, Ana.

ANA. I didn't enjoy it once, that's the truth.

EDWARD. Shhh…

EDWARD *puts a finger to her lips. She moves his hand away.*

ANA. Don't you want to know?

EDWARD. No.

ANA. You really don't want to know.

EDWARD. Honestly. No.

ANA opens her mouth to speak then stops herself.

EDWARD returns to doing up her buttons.

Again she puts a gentle hand on his cheek. Again he looks up at her.

ANA. I regret doing that to you.

EDWARD. I regret doing that to you.

They look at one another.

ANA. How will you ever trust me, how will I trust you?

EDWARD. Well, we just have to.

ANA. How?

EDWARD. We have to trust each other's intentions.

ANA. Our intentions?

EDWARD. Every day. All we have is our intentions.

ANA. And you would do that?

EDWARD. I would do that for you.

ANA. Why?

EDWARD. Because I love you.

ANA. Why?

EDWARD. I cannot tell you why.

ANA. Edward.

EDWARD. But if words mean that much to you, then let me be precise: I *intend* to love you always; I do not *intend* to hurt you or to fall in love with another; I do not *intend* to leave you for a younger woman, for any woman or man. I *intend* to use my intelligence to the service of my love. And, if all goes well, there is no reason why I wouldn't intend to love you for as long as we both shall live.

ANA *and* EDWARD *look at one another.*

Could you?

ANA. Intend to love you?

EDWARD *nods.*

Yes. Yes.

ANA *and* EDWARD *smile at one another.*

The End.

A Nick Hern Book

While You Lie first published in Great Britain as a paperback original in 2010 by Nick Hern Books Limited, The Glasshouse, 49a Goldhawk Road, London W12 8QP, in association with the Traverse Theatre, Edinburgh

Reprinted 2016

While You Lie copyright © 2010 Sam Holcroft

Sam Holcroft has asserted her right to be identified as the author of this work

Cover image: Claire Lams as Ana; photograph by Laurence Winram
Cover design: Ned Hoste, 2H

Typeset by Nick Hern Books, London
Printed in the UK by Mimeo Ltd, Huntingdon, Cambridgeshire PE29 6XX

A CIP catalogue record for this book is available from the British Library

ISBN 978 1 84842 124 0

Woodland
CARBON
www.woodlandcarbon.co.uk
NICK HERN BOOKS
Printed on Carbon Captured paper